Popcorn!

Elaine Landau

Illustrated by
Brian Lies

Charlesbridge

For Michael
          — E. L.

For the raccoon who raided my corn patch
          — B. L.

Text copyright © 2003 by Elaine Landau
Illustrations copyright © 2003 by Brian Lies

Published by Charlesbridge
85 Main Street, Watertown, MA 02472
(617) 926-0329
www.charlesbridge.com

Library of Congress Cataloging-in-Publication Data

Landau, Elaine.
  Popcorn / Elaine Landau; illustrated by Brian Lies.
  p. cm.
  ISBN 1-57091-442-7 (reinforced for library use)
  ISBN 1-57091-443-5 (softcover)
  1. Cookery (Popcorn)—Juvenile literature. 2. Popcorn—
Juvenile literature. I. Lies, Brian. II. Title.
  TX814.5.P66 L36 2003
  641.6'5677—dc21   2002002271

Printed in South Korea
(hc) 10 9 8 7 6 5 4 3 2 1
(sc) 10 9 8 7 6 5 4 3 2 1

The illustrations in this book were painted in acrylics.
The display type is set in Couchlover by CHANK and the text is
set in Sabon.
Color separations were made by Sung In Printing, South Korea
Printed and bound by Sung In Printing, South Korea
Production supervision by Brian G. Walker
Designed by Susan Mallory Sherman

Munching at the Movies

You're at the movies. You're next in line at the food counter. What are you about to ask for? If you said "popcorn," you're not alone. Each year Americans munch on 1,124,000 pounds of this crunchy, tasty treat. That's a lot of corn. It comes down to about 17.3 billion quarts, or about 68 quarts for every man, woman, and child!

A Special Kind of Corn

You've eaten popcorn. I'll bet you liked it, too. Otherwise you probably wouldn't be reading this book. But how much do you really know about popcorn? Let's find out. Pop quiz on popcorn.

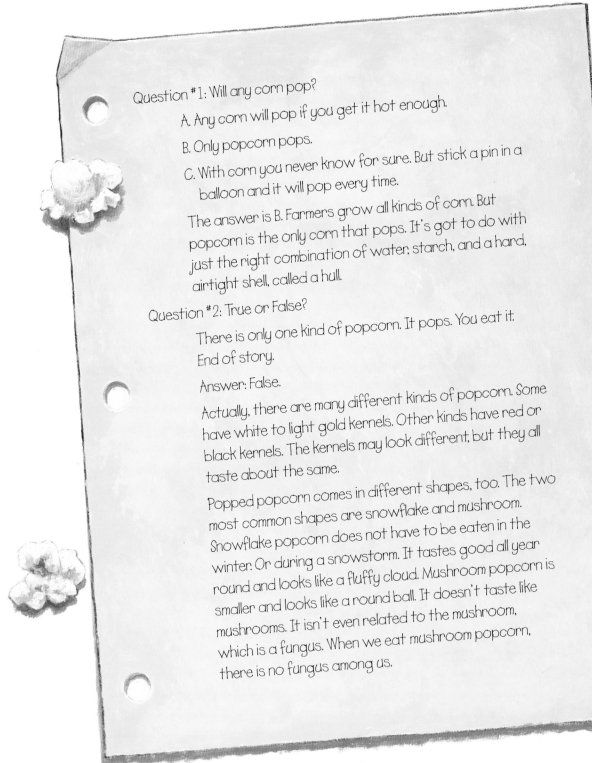

Question #1: Will any corn pop?

A. Any corn will pop if you get it hot enough.

B. Only popcorn pops.

C. With corn you never know for sure. But stick a pin in a balloon and it will pop every time.

The answer is B. Farmers grow all kinds of corn. But popcorn is the only corn that pops. It's got to do with just the right combination of water, starch, and a hard, airtight shell, called a hull.

Question #2: True or False?

There is only one kind of popcorn. It pops. You eat it. End of story.

Answer: False.

Actually, there are many different kinds of popcorn. Some have white to light gold kernels. Other kinds have red or black kernels. The kernels may look different, but they all taste about the same.

Popped popcorn comes in different shapes, too. The two most common shapes are snowflake and mushroom. Snowflake popcorn does not have to be eaten in the winter. Or during a snowstorm. It tastes good all year round and looks like a fluffy cloud. Mushroom popcorn is smaller and looks like a round ball. It doesn't taste like mushrooms. It isn't even related to the mushroom, which is a fungus. When we eat mushroom popcorn, there is no fungus among us.

4

Question #3: Where do people eat the most popcorn?

  A. At the movies

  B. At home

  C. Under the bed, hiding from hungry family members

The answer is B. Americans eat nearly three-quarters of their popcorn at home. Whether or not you hide under the bed is up to you. People eat the rest of their popcorn when they're out having fun. After all, popcorn is a fun food.

October is Popcorn Popping Month in the United States. People celebrate the harvest every fall with popcorn parties.

POPCORN FESTIVAL TODAY

Where Does Popcorn Come From?

Farmers plant popcorn kernels using corn-planting machines, called row planters, that drop them about two inches apart. Yes, these are the same kernels you'd put in a popcorn popper. That's because the kernels are the popcorn plant's seeds.

One to three weeks after planting, a sprout pushes its way out of the seed. The sprout grows into a green cornstalk between six and eight feet tall. Its long slender leaves sway in the wind. It takes about six months for corn to grow. Other leaves called husks cover the ear of corn itself.

Popcorn's scientific name is *Zea mays everta*. But don't try asking for that at the candy counter the next time you're at the movies. The clerk may tell you they don't have any.

Having an ear doesn't mean that the cornstalk can hear. Otherwise you'd have to be very careful what you said in cornfields. An ear of corn is made up of the cob and rows of kernels. By covering the ear, the husks protect the kernels that you'll later pop and eat.

Growing corn has to be protected from all kinds of pests that would like to feast, including deer, crows, and raccoons.

It's hard to believe as you picture a fluffy piece of popcorn, but all types of corn are members of the grass family. If you stand in a cornfield, everything around you looks green, like giant blades of grass.

Corn grows best in an area of the United States called the Corn Belt. No, it's not a real belt. You can't wear it around your waist. People call it that because it sort of looks like a belt on a map. The states in the Corn Belt are Indiana, Nebraska, Ohio, Illinois, Iowa, Missouri, Kentucky, and Michigan.

What makes the Corn Belt a good place to grow popcorn?

1. The soil is rich and deep. You want lots of nice, black dirt for your popcorn.

2. The area has perfect popcorn-growing weather. That means really warm days and gentle rain throughout the growing season, which lasts from late April or early May until late September or early October, when the popcorn is picked. That may seem like a long time to wait for your popcorn, but the taste is worth the wait.

e Corn Belt

STARCH

MOISTURE

OUTER
HULL

What Makes Popcorn Pop?

A jack-in-the-box pops. Bubble wrap pops.
And pop goes the weasel. But what makes popcorn
pop? The answer is simple: Water. Each kernel of
popcorn contains a droplet of water that came from
the soil when the popcorn plant was growing.
The droplet is surrounded by a circle of soft starch,
surrounded by the kernel's hard outer hull.
When you heat the kernel, the water expands and
turns into steam. That's what water does when it
gets really hot.

Pressure from the expanding steam builds up against the hard, airtight shell until POW, BAM, BOOM! The shell gives way, the soft starch explodes outward, turning the kernel inside out, and you have popped popcorn.

If you make your own popcorn, remember to protect its popability. Popcorn kernels need just the right amount of water inside them to pop, so never let leftover kernels dry out. Keep them in an airtight container in a cool place. Don't store unpopped kernels in the refrigerator or freezer. It's too dry in there.

Ideally, 98 percent of the kernels in any popcorn batch should pop. What about the kernels that don't—the ones you find at the bottom of the bowl or bag? They don't pop because they don't have the right amount of water inside, or because the outer hull of the kernel is damaged so that the heated water can escape without building up pressure.

People call these kernels old maids. But don't get your hopes up. These maids won't clean up after you.

Of course, you don't have to make your own popcorn. You can buy already-popped popcorn in supermarkets, gourmet candy stores, and popcorn shops that sell absolutely nothing other than popcorn! You can get cookies-and-cream popcorn, key-lime-pie popcorn, and pistachio popcorn (it's green!). There are also special holiday flavors. You can have cranberry popcorn on Thanksgiving and eggnog popcorn for Christmas. But you can't get smelly-shoe popcorn to trick your little brother. Not yet, anyway.

13

A Food with History

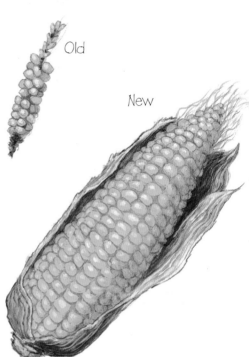

Old

New

Researchers have found 1,000-year-old grains of popcorn. That's older than anyone you know—including your teacher. These ancient grains were uncovered in tombs on the east coast of Peru. Believe it or not, the kernels still popped. How's that for popability?

But popcorn's history goes back even further than that. The oldest known ears of popcorn were discovered in a cave in New Mexico. They were about 5,600 years old. Popcorn ears were smaller back before modern scientists came up with ways to make them bigger. The ancient ears were less than two inches long—about the size of your pinky finger.

Originally, popcorn grew only in North and
South America, so most of the world didn't find out
about it until after Columbus came to America. But
Native Americans grew popcorn long before that.
Different Native American groups developed
different ways to eat popcorn.

The Iroquois of the Great Lakes region popped popcorn in special jugs that they placed in heated sand. The jugs allowed the popcorn to be heated evenly and stopped the popcorn from flying around. The Iroquois made popcorn soup with their corn.

HOT HOT HOT HOT HOT

Some Native Americans elsewhere spread oil
on ears of popcorn and placed them near a fire. The
kernels popped while still attached to the ears. It was
like eating corn on the cob, but with popcorn!

The Winnebago pushed sharp sticks through
their popcorn ears. Then they held them over a fire
the way you might roast hot dogs.

Native American Tales and Ceremonies

Some Native Americans told tales about why popcorn pops. They said that spirits lived inside each popcorn kernel. If you left them alone, the spirits remained quiet and happy. But they became angry if their houses got too hot. The hotter their homes became, the angrier the spirits would get. Finally, they would burst out of their houses and fly off into the air as annoyed puffs of steam.

The Aztecs used to scatter popcorn before a statue of Tlaloc, their water god, to protect fishermen during storms. The corn represented hailstones. The Aztecs also made popcorn headdresses, bracelets, and necklaces that they wore for special events or on holy days. They put the same popcorn ornaments on statues of their gods. Popcorn was more to them than a great-tasting food.

Popcorn at the First Thanksgiving?

Some people think that popcorn was served at the first Thanksgiving. One story says that the Native Americans brought a deerskin bag of popcorn to the feast as a gift for the colonists, who had never tasted this food. But people who study this stuff say it never happened. They claim that corn wasn't grown in the area until much later. Too bad—popcorn would have been a welcome treat that day. The colonists had used up their supply of flour, so there were no cakes or cookies. Just boiled pumpkin for dessert. In time, the colonists did get to taste popcorn. But instead of eating it as a dessert or snack, they put it in a bowl with water or milk and sugar. Presto! The first breakfast cereal was born. The popcorn got kind of mushy in all that liquid, but the colonists seemed to like it.

Popcorn Hits the Big Time

In the late 1880s, men were hired to pop popcorn in front of stores to draw in customers. These men were called poppers. Poppers were great for business.

The first popcorn "machines" were invented in 1885. They were designed to attract attention. The new machines looked like oversized glass cabinets with a kettle inside for popping popcorn. People could watch their snack being heated and popped. The machines could be pushed on foot, pulled by horses, or mounted on trucks so that the poppers could get closer to the crowds.

During the Great Depression of the 1930s, many Americans lost their jobs. Few had money for extras. But popcorn cost less than 10 cents a bag, so it was a tasty treat that people could afford. While other businesses went under, popcorn makers kept popping along.

Popcorn sales also boomed during World War II. American soldiers who had been sent overseas needed lots of supplies, and sugar was in high demand. That left American candy manufacturers without a key ingredient. The result was a national candy shortage. Popcorn to the rescue! Snack lovers devoured it instead of candy. Americans actually ate three times more popcorn than usual during the war.

According to *The Guinness Book of World Records*, the world's largest popcorn ball measured 12 feet wide. It contained 2,000 pounds of popcorn; 40,000 pounds of sugar; 280 gallons of corn syrup; and 400 gallons of water.

YUM!

Yet in the 1950s, popcorn sales dropped. A new invention known as television had become popular. Many Americans stayed home watching TV instead of going to the movies, and remember where a great deal of popcorn has always been eaten?

The slump changed once people began popping popcorn at home. Both pan popping and electric popping became commonplace. Home popping got even faster when microwave ovens became popular in the 1980s. Microwave popcorn was an instant hit! People still watched TV—but now they often ate popcorn while watching.

In fact you can eat popcorn while reading this book! Go get some. It's okay. I'll wait. . . .

Now that you've got your snack, it's time to let you in on a secret. Popcorn doesn't just taste good—it's good for you!

Popcorn is a wonderful source of carbohydrates, which give your body energy. But unlike other carbohydrates, such as chips or cookies, popcorn is sugar free and nearly fat free. Popcorn has more protein and iron than many other snack foods. Protein helps you grow. Iron helps form red blood cells, which travel through your body delivering oxygen and removing waste.

Popcorn is also a great source of fiber, which helps your digestive system. Lots of important people such as the National Cancer Institute and the American Dietetic Association cite popcorn as a healthy food choice. But the real judges have also weighed in—kids everywhere will tell you that popcorn is terrific!

Poppin' Popcorn

Popcorn kernels burst into the air like rockets fired into space. But you don't have to be a rocket scientist to pop popcorn. It's simple and fun. So get ready to make the best pan-popped popcorn this side of Jupiter.

Popcorn pops best between 400 and 460 degrees Fahrenheit. That's pretty hot. So it's smart to pop popcorn with an adult's help.

- With an adult's help, warm a pan on the stove.
- Add enough cooking oil to cover the bottom of the pan. Any cooking oil will do, but never use butter for popping popcorn. It burns. In this case, butter isn't better.
- Pour in the unpopped kernels. Be sure to put in enough kernels to cover the bottom of the pan, but don't let the kernels stack up.
- Cover the pan and shake it gently so the oil coats all the kernels. Soon you'll hear the kernels popping.
- After you've heard the last few pops, add a little salt. Don't get impatient and add the salt too early. Salting unpopped kernels toughens the popcorn.
- Pour the popcorn into a bowl and dig in. You'd better get a big bowl. When popped, popcorn kernels expand to about 40 times their original size!

You can also make popcorn in an electric popcorn popper. Just pour in the kernels, plug in the machine, and don't forget the bowl! Microwave popcorn is even easier to make. But electric poppers and microwave ovens use extremely hot temperatures, too, so ask for an adult's help with these. While you're at it, ask the adult to clean your room. You might get lucky.

Cooking hint: Two tablespoons of unpopped kernels make one quart of popped popcorn.

Popcorn Here, Popcorn There,

Lots of popcorn is grown each year in the United States. I really mean lots. Nearly 498,000 tons of it! Americans never seem to tire of popcorn. Did you know that more popcorn is eaten in the United States than anywhere else on Earth?

In China, early in the 20th century, street vendors popped popcorn outside just like the first American poppers. There was one big difference, though. The customers—usually children—would bring their own corn to be popped. You can still buy popcorn on the

Popcorn Poppin' Everywhere

street in China, but now you don't have to bring your own corn.

In some Russian towns you might see big bags of popcorn outside people's homes. The people selling it work in popcorn factories. Sometimes part of the workers' salary is paid in popcorn. They eat some and sell the rest.

And there you have it: the facts about popcorn. Now pop in on your friends and amaze them with particularly precise and pleasurable popcorn points.

RUSSIA

JAPAN ‡ CHINA

OVER HERE!

U.S. popcorn is exported to over 90 countries.

How Do You Eat Your Popcorn?

Many people only eat popcorn with butter and salt on it. Why limit yourself? Check out these snacking suggestions:

Super Savory Sprinkles

Try pouring one of these over your popcorn.
- Grated cheese
- Ranch or Italian salad dressing mix (use a little bit of vegetable oil to make it stick!)
- Cinnamon and sugar
- Seasoned salt
- Taco seasoning mix

Perfect Popcorn Partners

Mix these in with your popcorn.
- Nuts—peanuts, walnuts, almonds, or your favorite!
- Dried fruit, like raisins or cranberries
- Chow mein noodles or other crunchy snacks
- Chocolate chips (stick them in the freezer first so they don't melt!)

WARNING: Avoid these Crummy Corn Companions

- Brussels sprouts
- Caviar
- Paste
- Chewing gum
- Your little brother's science project festering in the fridge

Post-Popcorn Protocol

Open wide and put your toothbrush on turbo. Don't forget to floss, floss, floss. Those kernel bits can really burrow in deep!

Tasty Treat: Popcorn Balls

1. With an adult's help, combine one 16-ounce package of marshmallows and ¼ cup (that's half a stick) of butter or margarine in a large saucepan.
2. Cook over low heat until the mixture is completely melted. Keep stirring until it's totally smooth!
3. Place three quarts of popped popcorn in a large bowl and pour the melted mixture over it.
4. Let the popcorn cool for five minutes or so.
5. Then—and this is the fun part—grease your hands up with butter and shape the popcorn into balls.
6. Wrap the balls in waxed paper until you're ready to eat!

Hint: For an extra punch, add a few drops of food coloring to your marshmallow mixture before you pour it on the popcorn.

Some people even say that popcorn is a diet food. People who want to lose weight often snack on it. An eight-ounce bowl of plain popcorn—popped in oil—has about 55 calories. An eight-ounce bag of potato chips has about 150 calories. An eight-ounce bowl of French vanilla ice cream has about 349 calories. You do the math.

Resources

Here are some popular popcorn Web sites. Web sites can change, though, so try running a search on "popcorn" on your favorite search engine, too.

The Popcorn Board
http://www.popcorn.org
Packed with interesting popcorn info, this site offers a popcorn calendar and the Encyclopedia Popcornica.

Wyandot Popcorn Museum
http://www.wyandotpopcornmus.com
Visit the only popcorn museum in the world, featuring the largest collection of restored antique popcorn poppers.

The Marion (Ohio) Popcorn Festival
http://www.popcornfestival.com
This popcorn fair's been around for over 20 years! It's right nearby the Wyandot Popcorn Museum.

The Valparaiso (Indiana) Popcorn Festival
http://www.popcornfest.org
Orville Redenbacher established his first popcorn plant in this Midwestern town.

The Maize Page
http://maize.agron.iastate.edu
Learn all there is to know about popcorn's sister plant, maize—and check out a few popcorn facts along the way!

These books are good, too:

Bial, Raymond. *Corn Belt Harvest*. Boston: Houghton Mifflin, 1991.

Hunter, Sally M. *Four Seasons of Corn: A Winnebago Tradition*. Minneapolis: Lerner Publications, 1997.

Kudlinski, Kathleen V. *Popcorn Plants*. Minneapolis: Lerner Publications, 1998.

Miller, Jay. *American Indian Foods*. New York: Children's Press, 1996.

Seelig, Tina L. *Incredible Edible Science*. New York: Scientific American Books for Young Readers, 1994.

Woodside, Dave. *What Makes Popcorn Pop?* New York: Atheneum, 1980.